JESUITS
TELLING
JOKES

JESUITS TELLING JOKES

A

[SERIOUS]

Introduction

to Ignatian

Spirituality

NIKOLAAS SINTOBIN, SJ

With cartoons by Joris Snaet

LOYOLA PRESS.
A JESUIT MINISTRY
Chicago

LOYOLA PRESS.
A JESUIT MINISTRY

3441 N. Ashland Avenue
Chicago, Illinois 60657
(800) 621-1008
www.loyolapress.com

Original, Dutch edition: © NV Uitgeverij Altiora Averbode, 2013, text and illustrations under the title *Jezuïeten grappen*.

As indicated, all quotations from the *Spiritual Exercises* are taken from *Draw Me into Your Friendship: A Literal Translation and a Contemporary Reading of the Spiritual Exercises* by David L. Fleming, SJ (St. Louis: The Institute of Jesuit Sources, 1996) or *Understanding the Spiritual Exercises* by Michael Ivens, SJ (Herefordshire, England: Gracewing, 2004).

Cover art credit: mers1na/iStock/Thinkstock

ISBN-13: 978-0-8294-4373-8
ISBN-10: 0-8294-4373-8
Library of Congress Control Number: 2016945074

Printed in the United States of America.

16 17 18 19 20 21 22 Versa 10 9 8 7 6 5 4 3 2 1

Contents

Foreword

This little book is funny and serious at the same time. It describes in clear and engaging language how Jesuits live, pray, and work. It is an excellent introduction to the spirituality of the Jesuits, to their way of proceeding. Nikolaas Sintobin, himself a Jesuit, manages to combine good information with a fluent writing style. The story flows from his pen. You will learn a great deal about St. Ignatius of Loyola and the first Jesuits, but you will also learn just as much about who the Jesuits are today. In twenty concise chapters, Sintobin deals with essential aspects of Ignatian spirituality, such as life in the midst of tensions, the deeply intimate relationship with God, formation for freedom and social involvement, Jesuit obedience, and the guidance and direction of young people and adults, to mention just a few. You also may recognize some aspects of this spirituality in the things Pope Francis does and says—after all, it was the Jesuits who provided Pope Francis with his formation!

The author is deeply immersed in the Jesuit way of life. He has lived in many Jesuit communities and has worked as an educator in Paris and Antwerp for many years. He is a director of the Spiritual Exercises and is currently active as an Internet chaplain.

Sintobin begins each chapter in this book with a Jesuit joke. He brings both old and new to light by delving into the reservoir of jokes about religious orders. And maybe being able to laugh at themselves is a quality that the Jesuits possess. After all, humor helps enlarge one aspect of a person's life so that it becomes to some extent laughable. But that said, humor would never do any harm. Humor is, moreover, important for a healthy spiritual life, at least according to the famous *Dictionnaire de Spiritualité*, published by the French Jesuits. Nikolaas Sintobin is therefore in good company! Enjoy these Jesuit jokes and don't take them too seriously.

Mark Rotsaert, SJ
Pontifical Gregorian University, Rome

Who Are the Jesuits?

Who are those Catholic priests who were banned by the Pope at the end of the eighteenth century, only to find one of their own chosen as Pope two hundred and fifty years later?

We're about to find out through jokes about them. There are twenty Jesuit jokes in this book. Hopefully they provide a good laugh, but they're also intended to illuminate some realities about the Jesuits. Humor often manages to touch, in a very subtle way, the core of the mystery surrounding how people live and work. Humor can make you think. So humor is well-suited for shedding some light on an order that is nearly five centuries old.

Jokes about priests and the religious have been making the rounds for millennia, including those about Jesuits. The Jesuits have been compared to Franciscans, Dominicans, and many other orders. Some jokes may make fun of a Jesuit "superiority complex," but those times are over, especially after the Jesuit Pope Francis chose to take the name of the humble founder of the Franciscans.

The founder of the Jesuits, Saint Ignatius of Loyola (1491–1556), is often shown in paintings as ascetic, strong-willed, and icy-looking. He was ascetic and strong-willed, but those who knew him well give a subtler and more nuanced view of him. Luis Gonçalves da Câmara, a Jesuit who lived and worked with him, describes Ignatius as "a Spaniard, of small stature, rather lame, with joyful eyes." His friends talk about his sense of humor and capacity to make fun of himself.

Ignatius lived in a time of crisis, much as we do today. After centuries of religious stability, Europe was experiencing a period of religious uncertainty and fear. The discovery of highly developed cultures overseas led to doubts about Christian superiority, and new knowledge challenged established, centuries-old intellectual beliefs. In the midst of countless tensions that were the result of this rapid evolution, Ignatius went in search of meaning in his life. Little by little, he discovered that the all-too-easy answers he used to accept now required more discernment and nuances. Human reality doesn't fit into yes-or-no, black-or-white answers, and this complexity can be found in Ignatius's spirituality and pedagogy. His complex spirituality can even be nuanced to such an extent that the term "Jesuitical" has become fairly synonymous with being ambiguous or seemingly hypocritical.

It is clear that Ignatius had an aversion to black-and-white thinking. His fondness for discernment, or prayerfully reflecting on one's inner movements and emotions, meant that he loved paradoxes. His own history had led him to seek God in the fickle nature of concrete experiences rather than in devout thoughts or generalities. In this way, Ignatius laid the foundation for a spiritual tradition that both attracts and repels: It is unpredictable and yet still within the tradition; it is subtle and bold; it trusts in God and in human efforts.

This little book introduces you to various aspects of the Jesuit approach to life in twenty brief sections. I hope you will better understand who the Society of Jesus (the Jesuits) are and gain some insight into Ignatian spirituality, which offers sure guidance for developing a more meaningful life.

Special thanks to Hans Geybels, who gave me the idea for this book. I hope you enjoy it!

Nikolaas Sintobin, SJ

Finding God and Serving Him in All Things

A man goes to a Franciscan and asks him to say a novena for him so that he'll win a Lexus in a lottery.
"What's a Lexus?"
"It's a luxury car."
"Good heavens! Saint Francis loved poverty. Sorry, but I couldn't possibly pray for that."
Then the man went to a Dominican: "Please say a novena so that I can win a Lexus."
"What's a Lexus?"
"A luxury car."
"Oh, no! Saint Thomas Aquinas warned us against the love of worldly goods. Sorry, but I can't pray for something like that."
As a last resort, the man went to a Jesuit and asked him: "Please, Father, will you say a novena for me to win a Lexus?"
"What's a novena?"

St. Ignatius of Loyola (1491–1556) was a reformer, a man who updated a number of the traditional customs surrounding monastic and religious life within the Catholic Church. One of his most obvious reforms—considered scandalous at the time—was doing away with the common chanting/praying of the Liturgy of the Hours as a community. Unlike cloistered monks and most other religious of the time, Jesuits were not required to interrupt their activities several times a day to pray the Liturgy of the Hours in a chapel. Instead, they would organize their daily prayer individually, in consultation with their spiritual director. Ignatius also decided that Jesuits would wear more discreet clothing instead of the monastic "habit." Moreover, Jesuits wouldn't live in monasteries, separated and sometimes far from the world. Rather, they would live in ordinary houses among the townspeople.

Ignatius invites his companions to find God and to serve him in all things. In practice, this has led his followers to take up diverse and sometimes unexpected areas of ministry. Many Jesuits work in education or are involved in spirituality programs and spiritual guidance, while others work in prisons, as nurses, or as priests in local parishes. Jesuits also have contributed to academic disciplines such as astronomy, mathematics, and cartography. These days, you'll even find Jesuits specializing in ecology, the Internet, video production, business ethics, international politics, dance, and music of all kinds. The list is endless.

Jesuits are busy in many places that are not at all "churchy." Yet their fundamental goal is to help others "find God in all things"—making God's presence alive and relevant, something for people everywhere to think and talk about. This means that they are continually challenged to be fully present in the world, to wholeheartedly love the world, and yet, not become totally secular. It is hardly surprising that, as a result, many Jesuits do not have enough time for traditional monastic and devotional practices, however valuable they may be.

Living with Tensions

At the end of a conversation, a woman asked a Jesuit, "Father, is it true that a Jesuit will never give you a straight answer?"
He replied, "Well, yes and no . . ."

Ignatius lived in a time when almost all trusted religious, cultural, economic, and intellectual reference points were shifting. The extent of the known world had tripled within just a few decades, knowledge increased exponentially, and travel and trade expanded across the globe. The Reformation and subsequent Counter-Reformation in the 1500s brought an end to centuries of certainty and relative tranquillity. Change and uncertainty became the order of the day, opening up new possibilities. Ignatius was born into a world that showed many striking parallels to our own day and age.

His spirituality offers a guidebook for those trying to find their way within a continuously changing culture. Just as in the 1500s, we too live amid countless tensions—within the Church and our surrounding culture. Ignatius doesn't suggest that we should get rid of these tensions, for that would be neither possible nor desirable. Rather, Ignatius suggests that we should stand resolutely in the midst of all these tensions and allow ourselves to experience them. In this way, we can gradually learn to search for a subtle and continually changing balance in our lives.

Remaining open as we search for our path in life is tough to do. As illustrated in the joke above, most of us long for simple, black-and-white answers. We want to hear a clear yes or no—at least then we'll know where we stand. Or we might feel inclined to demand: "Just say what you think. Don't beat around the bush."

The Jesuit tradition works against these desires by inviting people to explore the different and often apparently contradictory or irreconcilable aspects of a problem when searching for a solution. Ignatius asks his companions to consider both sides of an argument. He reminds them that in the future they may have to work with the people whose beliefs and opinions are different from their own. Consequently, he gives the following advice: "If you are asked for anything you think it would be harmful to give, take care, though you refuse what is asked, to retain the asker's friendship."

Granted, being gentle with those who disagree with you can sometimes become very tiresome. It can also, on occasion, create the impression (not wholly unjustified!) that a Jesuit is inclined to hide behind all kinds of subtleties and doesn't have the courage to make a decision or stake a clear position. But surely, experience teaches us that a well-thought-out compromise is a solution offered by the wise person rather than the coward. Don't simplistic answers tend to trap people more than liberate them? A considered response can create space and trust in which something new can grow and creativity can thrive—a much better return than a straight answer.

Daring to Trust

A Franciscan and a Jesuit were friends. Both smokers, they found it difficult to pray for long without having a cigarette. They decided to ask their superiors for permission to smoke.

The next time they met, the Franciscan was downcast. "I asked my superior if I could smoke while I pray, and he said, 'No.'"

The Jesuit smiled. "I asked if I could pray while I smoke, and my superior said, 'Of course.'"

Ignatius demanded a lot from his brother Jesuits, especially from those who were the most gifted and whom he cared most about. He placed his faith and trust in others' talents and goodness. And he had good reason to—after all, doesn't the Bible remind us that we are created in the very image and likeness of God?

In the introductory section of his famous work, the *Spiritual Exercises*, Ignatius gives the following advice:

> In order that both he who is giving the Spiritual Exercises, and he who is receiving them, may more help and benefit themselves, let it be presupposed that every good Christian is to be more ready to save his neighbor's proposition than to condemn it. (*SE* 22, Fleming)

Jesuits have an extremely optimistic view of humanity, and they are often criticized for this. They are inclined to encourage people to have a great deal of personal freedom and responsibility. When in doubt, Jesuits are always willing to give someone another chance to get things right. Ignatius himself testifies to this: "Beware of condemning any man's action. Consider your neighbor's intention, which is often honest and innocent, even though his act seems bad in outward appearance."

This attitude explains why Ignatius was so concerned about protecting the good name of his fellow Jesuits. Pedro de Ribadeneira, SJ, who lived with Ignatius in the same community for many years and was his first biographer, explains:

> He watched over the good name and reputation of his fellow Jesuits with the utmost care, and he did this in two ways.
>
> Firstly, he always spoke positively about them and showed that he held them all in great esteem. He never made anyone's mistakes public, except when necessity demanded that he seek advice in order to conquer evil. Even in such a case, he would not discuss matters with two people if one person's advice proved sufficient. If he needed to consult with two people, he wouldn't ask a third. He would explain the issue without exaggerating anything.

Secondly he would severely chastise those who spoke ill of their companions or caused others to have a less favorable opinion of them. For example, it happened that a good and saintly old man was told to pray three psalms as penance for having gossiped outside the house, because he'd told how a fellow priest had said some crazy things in a moment of anger.

It is possible, of course, that some will take advantage of this level of trust in others. It's also possible that this method of giving someone the benefit of the doubt can go wrong. But if someone doesn't have the courage to take that risk, he'd be better off staying at home in bed! Especially for the young, there is nothing that helps them grow more in self-confidence and self-worth than being trusted by others. Young people in particular find true freedom when they are trusted and learn to deal with the consequent responsibilities. It's important to take everyone's age and capacity into consideration, but the younger a person is when he begins, the better. And of course, we need to accept that difficult and frustrating experiences are part of this process.

Trusting others requires most of all that you take the person's "deepest desires" seriously. Ignatius had discovered in prayer that he could meet God in his own heart. He therefore invited his fellow Jesuits to talk openly and completely about their deepest desires and longings. As much as possible, he took their hopes and dreams into consideration when deciding what work they would do. Ignatius invites us all to truly listen to others. However inarticulately, what are they really trying to tell us? We know too well that there are no silly questions, just silly answers. Truly listening to those around us will always be a fascinating challenge.

Freedom in Obedience

At a conference on the Vow of Obedience, someone asked a Jesuit, "How do you ensure that Jesuits remain faithful to this vow? I know that the Jesuits place great emphasis on this vow."

The Jesuit replied, "It's simple. First, our superiors ask us what we want to do, and then they tell us to do it. We never have any problems with obedience!"

Another conference participant was curious and asked him, "But surely there must be some Jesuits who don't know what they want to do? What do you do with them?"

The Jesuit replied, "Oh, that's easy. We make them our superiors!"

Obedience is a highly regarded tradition in the Society of Jesus. "The greater the obedience, the greater the freedom," is not just a casual remark made about Jesuit obedience. A Jesuit's religious vow is, first and foremost, an obedience to his vocation: to follow whatever God is inviting that Jesuit to do. The superior plays an important role in how the Vow of Obedience is experienced, and this is as true of a local community superior as it is of national or international Jesuit leaders.

Jesuits embrace a tradition known as the "account of conscience." Once a year the provincial superior visits each of his communities in order to speak privately with each Jesuit.

More precisely, every community member explains his insights and deeper experiences, his joys and sorrows, hopes, desires, and fears to the provincial, revealing everything in complete and utter trust. Jesuits view this experience as more of a privilege than an imposed obligation. A Jesuit can open up the deepest part of his heart to a fellow Jesuit, without fear of being judged or evaluated.

It is no coincidence that the same provincial superior is responsible for assigning each Jesuit to a particular work in his province. Taking the account of conscience as the basis for his decision, the provincial will, whenever possible, assign each Jesuit to a mission that fits his desires, strengths, and limitations. Of course, sometimes this isn't possible because some jobs just have to be filled. And often, obedience to this assignment can be gut-wrenchingly difficult, but it can also be liberating. Centuries of experience have shown that obedience enables Jesuits to find themselves capable of things that they otherwise would have believed impossible. Jesuits call this the "grace of state."

Though Ignatius believed that obedience is the one virtue Jesuits should excel in, he did not believe in blind obedience. Jesuits have the right of "representation." A Jesuit has the right and obligation to "represent" his thoughts and feelings to his superior if, in all honesty and in accordance with his conscience, he finds it too difficult to accept a mission he's been given. If necessary, he can repeat his objections a second or third time, while accepting that the superior ultimately has the last word.

Within a Jesuit community, the superior has a key role. His primary task is to work humbly in the service of others, even to the extent of putting his own apostolic work to the side in order to help his fellow Jesuits grow in their vocations and missions. In principle, the superior's term is limited to six years, after which he will receive a new mission just like every other Jesuit.

Ignatius had high expectations for Jesuit obedience, which is why he dealt with obedience issues cautiously and with great sensitivity. Luis Gonçalves da Câmara, SJ, writes:

> Our Father is accustomed to do all that he can gently without recourse to obedience. On the contrary, when something can be done without knowing what is the Superior's preference, but by personal choice, this pleases him more. And when someone undertakes an action because he has perceived the preference of the Superior, but has not been ordered to undertake it, he is more pleased than if he had been obliged to order it, and finally for the same reason, when the action is taken under orders, but not by virtue of obedience.

5

The Discernment of Spirits

There are three things that even God doesn't know about the Church:
1) Exactly how many congregations of religious women there are.
2) The amount of money that the Franciscans have stashed away.
3) What the Jesuits really think and what they are going to do next.

Ignatian spirituality is not doctrinal. It is hardly, if at all, concerned with knowledge, and even less so with secrets. Jesuits do work according to a plan, but they also have what they call their own "way of proceeding"—*modo de proceder* in the words of Ignatius—a method they describe as the "discernment of spirits."

While confined to his sickbed in Loyola, Spain, Iñigo (the name by which Ignatius was then known) experienced God making himself known through "movements" in his heart during prayer. Very gradually, Iñigo learned to discern how the Holy Spirit spoke to him through fluctuations between joy and sadness, tranquillity and restlessness. He also learned how he could use these insights about discernment when making significant life choices.

One of the great contributions Ignatius made to Christianity was his development of a systematic method for refining discernment and, to the extent it was possible, making it concrete. Ignatius formalized this method in his twenty-two Rules for the Discernment of Spirits in the *Spiritual Exercises*, a bedrock Jesuits rely upon to this day to make fundamental choices and decisions.

We are unable, however, to predict God's will and desire for us. Jesuits, therefore, consciously seek inner freedom so they are ready to respond to the promptings of the Holy Spirit—even if doing so can sometimes be uncomfortable. For, when it comes down to it, most of us like certainty and prefer to be the ones running the show. We love knowing in advance what is expected of us, and it can be difficult to be patient and attune and open to God's plan.

In 2008, 225 Jesuits gathered in Rome to choose the twenty-ninth successor to Ignatius. That took place, in accordance with tradition, by means of a process of fasting and prayerful discernment over a period of several days. When the Jesuits went into seclusion, the delegates refused to have a list of possible candidates made known to them. Peter-Hans Kolvenbach, SJ, the general superior who was stepping down, had compiled the list on the basis of names put forward by representatives from every continent. The delegates, however, wished to discern without any prejudice and with completely open minds in a process of dynamic communal discernment in order to recognize God's desire.

Ignatius, a devoted companion of Jesus with outstanding faith in God, was such a master in discernment that it became second nature to him. He was prepared to take whatever time was necessary. Twenty years lay between his conversion and the founding of the Society of Jesus, and during these years, Ignatius and his companions discerned step-by-step what God was inviting them to do. Jerome Nadal, SJ, his confidant and spokesman, describes his approach as follows:

> Ignatius, his heart simply focused on Christ, followed the Holy Spirit without passing Him by and so he was gently led towards the unknown; and gradually the way was opened up to him, which he wisely took.

6

Experiencing and Discovering for Ourselves

A student asked a Jesuit whether it was true that Jesuits always answer a question with another question.
The Jesuit looked at the young man and said, "What do you mean?"

Answering one question with another—anyone with teaching experience has used this technique, knowing it cannot be ignored when it comes to a student's growth. It has become one of psychotherapy's fundamental tactics, and conscientious parents know about it too. St. Ignatius, a born educator, was applying this technique in the sixteenth century. He understood that whatever someone learns on her own, whatever she discovers for herself, whatever she puts into her own words and expresses has a much deeper impact than an answer presented on a golden plate, eloquently solved by someone else, even if it looks or sounds quite wonderful.

During their long and extensive formation, Jesuits acquire a lot of knowledge. Their knowledge is a strength, but it also carries formidable risk. There is little merit to be found in presenting oneself as more learned than others, whether those persons are younger or older. And it's even worse to squash someone else with what you know or can do. Making yourself the center of attention won't get you anywhere in the long run. That is even more the case when you're engaged with the formation and guidance of people.

The Jesuits' dealings with people entrusted to us for the purposes of education or guidance only begin to be truly fascinating when we are prepared to put the other person first and show a willingness to learn ourselves. With this trust and openness, a student or participant will find the incentive to grow in both word and action. For example, we learn to ice-skate better and quicker when we get onto the unfamiliar and slippery ice. We'll experience the joys of learning to stand up and skate on our own two feet. Even with appropriate guidance, we'll still have our ups and downs.

The Jesuits' way of proceeding can be met with amazement or even resistance, not least by the person on the receiving end of the instruction. In the short run, spiritual directors or teachers may feel a greater comfort and satisfaction when they can give ready-made answers to young people who show an eagerness to learn. They'll also have a secure feeling they can give good advice to those seeking spiritual guidance, clarifying for them what is happening in their heart and soul. And yet Jesuits will often prefer to remain silent, especially within the framework of spiritual guidance and direction. The challenge is, after all, to teach others to take charge of their own lives.

Knowing when to withdraw in a conscious and well-thought-out way requires a continuous attentiveness, expertise, and delicate sensitivity on the part of the educator or spiritual director. It also demands humility, self-denial, and patience—particularly if the person leading thinks he or she knows what's better for someone else and could solve the problem faster and more efficiently. Yet, if the leader really wants to allow the other person to develop, he or she must be ready to say less, even to remain silent and withdraw. The result will be a mutual learning process that will enrich both parties.

In other words, within the Ignatian tradition, education and spiritual direction are not only concerned with passing on knowledge, important as this is, but also with enhancing the formation of a person's character. Even though a teacher is an expert in the subject he or she is teaching, data transfer is not the main task. Teaching is much more about the learner's personal growth.

This fundamental attitude of mutual respect must be applied even more strictly when a person is making a decision about his or her life choices. In this situation, the Jesuit spiritual director's diffident reticence will be all the more important. At times, the person receiving direction may attach too much importance to the inclinations of the director when their relationship is one of deep trust. Experience shows, however, that a person can only be truly faithful to his or her choice if it has been made in complete freedom. To be even more precise, a decision truly comes from God when the person has listened to that inner voice speaking through the deepest desires of his or her heart. For this reason, Ignatius gives the following advice to those who direct the Spiritual Exercises, shown here in two different translations:

> The giver of the Exercises should not be swayed or show a preference for one side of a choice rather than the other, but remaining in the centre like the pointer of a balance should leave the Creator to deal with the creature, and the creature with the Creator and Lord. (*SE* 15, Ivens)

> He who is giving the Exercises should not turn or incline to one side or the other, but standing in the center like a balance, leave the Creator to act immediately with the creature, and the creature with its Creator and Lord. (*SE* 15, Fleming)

On the Path of Excellence

A Jesuit, a Dominican, and a Franciscan were walking along, debating the greatness of their orders, when suddenly a vision of the Holy Family appeared, with Jesus in a manger and Mary and Joseph praying over him. The Franciscan prostrated himself, overcome at the sight of God born into such poverty.

The Dominican fell to his knees, adoring the beautiful scene of the Holy Family.

The Jesuit walked up to Joseph, put his arm around his shoulder, and said, "So, have you given any thought about which school you'll send him to?"

When Ignatius Loyola and his companions founded the Society of Jesus in 1539, they had no plans to found schools or colleges. Ignatius's ideal was that the Jesuits, like the apostles, would be pilgrims traveling from place to place. (It's difficult to imagine them embracing the stable life of a teacher.) However, by the time of Ignatius's death in 1556, the Jesuits had founded about fifty schools. Even in those days, times were changing fast! Today, there are about four thousand educational institutions worldwide with links to the Society of Jesus. Jesuits have always had strong connections with both education and formation, and the key to this involvement is found in their spirituality, particularly in the Spiritual Exercises.

You could say that Ignatian pedagogy has developed to a very large extent from the relationship that exists between the director and the person making the Spiritual Exercises, which, in a large point, parallels the relationship between educators and students. In the *Spiritual Exercises*, Ignatius gives tips to the spiritual director—and to the educator, when extending this to education—on how the director should guide the person making the Exercises. We have already considered the necessity of taking a discreet and modest stance so that a young person can grow, and we have dealt with how positively the Jesuits view those on the Exercises, as well as the important role of trust in Ignatian pedagogy.

But we haven't dealt with one of the fundamentals of Ignatian pedagogy and teaching: the unique path of growth that each person is invited to take. As Ignatius says, "It is dangerous to make everybody go forward by the same road: and worse to measure others by oneself." Educating young people does not mean forcing them into previously formed molds. Rather, Ignatian spirituality encourages spiritual directors and educators to avoid making any specific choices for young people or imposing their own experiences of success on students.

The successful educator directs, guides, and enables young people to discover for themselves their deepest desires about their future—desires God places in the heart of each person.

As Ignatius taught, if we learn to graft our choices, large or small, onto the vine of our deepest desires, then we will continue to develop and grow. A human being's potential is virtually unlimited—and this goes for every human person, regardless of his or her age, for the student just as much as for the teacher. Some people's gifts may be in sports or the creative arts, for others, in an intellectual or a religious field. No one is condemned to mediocrity. Those who live their lives from the wellspring of their deepest desire will find a way to push back the boundaries. Of course, there will be moments when one must find the strength to accept necessary boundaries and limitations, their own and sometimes those of others. This is also a source of personal integration and growth.

Authentic excellence implies going beyond one's own boundaries to take on responsibility for others. Pedro Arrupe, SJ, a former General Superior of the Jesuits, called this educating young people to become "men and women for others." Ignatian excellence, then, is not about marching orders. Neither is it a license to devote your life to sculpting or painting a work of art that is just for yourself. Authentic excellence takes us from egocentricity toward "other-centering," toward following the example of Jesus.

Excelling in something, as Ignatius understood it, is only fully liberating when it originates from love. At the end of the *Spiritual Exercises*, Ignatius writes: "Love ought to find its expression in deeds rather than in words." And immediately afterwards: "Love consists in mutual communication." That is to say the lover gives and communicates to the loved one what they have, or something of what they have, or are able to give; and in turn the one loved does the same for the lover. (*SE* 230–231, Ivens)

> Love ought to be put more in deeds than in words. . . . Love consists in interchange between two parties; that is to say in the lover's giving and communicating to the beloved what he has or out of what he has or can; and so, on the contrary, the beloved to the lover. (*SE* 230–231, Fleming)

8

Moving from the Fifth Gospel to the Peripheries

A mother goes to her pastor and explains that her son seems very interested in becoming a priest. She'd like to know what this entails. The priest begins to explain, "If he wants to become a diocesan priest, he'll have to study for eight years. If he wants to become a Franciscan, he'll have to study for ten years. If he wants to become a Jesuit, he'll have to study for fourteen years."

The mother listens carefully, and as the priest concludes, her eyes brighten. "Sign him up for that last one, Father—he's a little slow!"

Jesuits are well known for the long formation they receive. Besides the usual philosophy and theology studies for the priesthood, many also undertake secular studies and participate in a wide variety of internships during their training.

Jesuits work willingly in the heart of the Church, but more often you'll find them on the peripheries of the Church, in places you wouldn't expect: in the sciences, the arts, the media, and in dialogue with political dissidents or with people of other faiths.

Specialized knowledge can be a requirement for such work. After all, if a Jesuit wishes to be taken seriously by his fellow scientists and other partners in dialogue, then he must be able to speak as an equal. Faith is a huge grace and strength, but the ability to reason and knowledge itself are also gifts from God. Precisely because of this, Jesuits are encouraged to develop these gifts and use them effectively. St. Teresa of Avila, a contemporary of Ignatius and a mystic, said that if she had to choose between a saintly confessor and a learned confessor, she would choose the learned confessor.

Ignatian spirituality is based on the premise that we can love and serve God in all things. Following in the footsteps of Ignatius, Jesuits and many other Christians try to become more sensitive to God's presence in all things. They do this not only in prayer and in liturgy, but in all possible everyday matters. This explains why Jesuits do not recoil from committing themselves to long and drawn-out meditations. They apply themselves to very ordinary matters with the same commitment.

Just consider the numerous Jesuit lay brothers who have borne witness to this for centuries by living out their religious calling in humble and often unacknowledged household tasks. Or Jesuits who live out their calling through secular work such as architecture, administration, or scientific research. They are the living proof that everyday life can be both the place where you seek God and the place where you find him, and not less so than when offering Mass. There are no human activities that are doomed to be commonplace.

This particular way of living one's life touches the very core of Jesuit spirituality. Jesuits refer to it as, in the words of Ignatius's spokesman, Jerónimo Nadal, SJ, "contemplatives in action," or a practice of being reflective and prayerful as a person engages with God and the world. In order to train yourself in being a contemplative in action, Ignatius recommended the Examen prayer, also known as the Daily Examen or the Consciousness Examen. In the past it was better known as the Examen of Conscience.

The Examen is very simple. It is a prayerful review of the day, performed retrospectively, and can be done in three steps. You begin by thanking God (*thank you*) for his active presence in your life: for all that was beautiful, for all that made you happy and filled you with a sense of trust. Sometimes there will be big things, but mostly it will be about small, apparently insignificant events. There is nothing that points more preeminently to God's presence in our lives than joy, certainly when it's lasting joy, which is why thanking God is the most important step of the Examen.

The second step is to ask for forgiveness (*sorry*) for all the times in the day when you didn't do the right thing. Usually these are large or small experiences that have left behind an unpleasant aftertaste. These instances are more an indication of God's absence or of our exclusion of him during the day. From this more accentuated state of awareness of light and dark in your life, you will be ready for the third step, to ask God for the strength you need for the following day (*please*).

The Examen is also sometimes referred to as praying with the "fifth gospel," or praying with the story of God in your own life. You can pray the Examen in just five minutes before you go to sleep at night or devote an hour to it. You can pray it in the quiet of a chapel or while walking or driving a car. Either way, you'll gain more awareness, because you will be living connected to God and in union with him.

Constantly Adapting

A man had three sons who entered three different religious orders: the eldest became a Dominican, the second a Franciscan, and the youngest a Jesuit. On his deathbed, the father said to his sons, "I know you have all taken a vow of poverty, but as a sign of your love for me, I want each one of you to place one thousand dollars in my casket to be buried with me." On the day of the funeral, the Dominican son stepped up, placed $1,000 in the coffin, and said, "This seems like a waste of money, since you can't take it with you, Dad. But with the special permission of my superiors, I'm doing as you requested, as a sign of my love."

Next, the Franciscan son approached the coffin and said, "You know I love you, Dad, but the needs of the poor are so great, I just can't let $1,000 be buried with you. I hope you understand, now that you are in heaven. Please forgive me."

Finally, the Jesuit son came forward and said to his brother, "Don't worry, Frank. I'll pay your share." Then he reached into the coffin, took out the cash left by his eldest brother, and put in a check for $3,000.

Ignatius could be very strict. As general superior, he often gave detailed instructions in highly specified documents about procedures that had to be followed. However, it was also well known that *adaptation* was his favorite word.

Clear rules and detailed instructions can bring freedom. They protect against subjectivity, the whim of the moment, and guarantee greater justice. However, if no one is willing to adapt, the rules can quickly degenerate and cause injustice. Remaining faithful to the instructions is very different from blindly following the letter of the law—responsible creativity and flexibility are required. Even when two situations seem similar, it is sometimes necessary to come up with very different solutions.

Ignatius invited us to be constantly aware of the context in which events took place. A certain context could mean that we have to consider a different response to problems that, at first sight, may seem very similar in nature. What Jesuits refer to as *cura personalis*—attention and care for the entire person—is closely associated with this. As parents and educators know all too well, what may be beneficial for one child can sometimes be destructive for another. Discerning love demands continual attention, awareness, and creative courage of each person's situation.

Pedro de Ribadeneira, SJ, the first official biographer of Ignatius of Loyola, explains how the founder of the Jesuits practiced cura personalis:

> If he, in a particular case, made an exception, he would neither tolerate people becoming annoyed about it nor people telling him that it might cause annoyance. Neither would

he allow that someone else who did not need it, should request or desire the same exception to be made for themselves. Because it would indicate a lack of discernment, according to his mind, to measure unequal things with the same measuring stick, and it would be a disorderly deed to, without good reason, lay claim to a rule based on an exception, which was only permitted to the others as a matter of necessity.

For a superior it would be a weakness and contrary to love, to deny someone the very thing he needed because of the fear of complaints and protests, or to avoid requests for the same by people who did not need it. The norm in these matters should never be left to whim and the wishes of each individual, but be based on an actual need, determined by the wise and gentle love of the superior.

The Ministry of Silence

During a retreat for priests, the retreat director asked everyone to break up into groups of three. They were then asked to share their deepest, darkest secrets with one another, things they had never shared with anyone else before.

A Dominican, after much hesitation, told the other two in his group that he was an alcoholic. He'd been ashamed to tell anyone that he drank all the time and just couldn't kick the habit. He was glad he could share this in the safety of this small group and now felt better and freer.

A Franciscan also hesitated, but, sure he could trust the other two, told them that his problem was gambling. He was unable to control his urge to gamble and was deeply in debt. He was very ashamed of this habit but grateful he could finally share it with fellow priests.

It was the Jesuit's turn. He thanked them for their openness and honesty, admitting that he, too, was ashamed by his own problem. He'd been working on it for years but hadn't yet gotten it under control. Despite hypnosis and other therapies, nothing had helped him overcome his compulsion to gossip.

"When you say anything in secret, speak as if you were speaking to the whole world." This quote from St. Ignatius shows that he knew only too well that confidentiality is a rare commodity in our world.

And in spiritual direction or a spiritual dialogue, a ministry at the heart of each Jesuit's vocation, confidentiality and trust are necessary. Participants in spiritual direction open their hearts to Jesuits in their search to lead lives more in tune with the gospel, and when they are faced with an important decision or reach a turning point in their lives, absolute trust and discretion are required.

Rather than dominating the conversation, a Jesuit will try to create the space needed during spiritual direction for the person to speak freely. He won't fish for spicy details; instead he'll encourage the other person to describe how situations and events resonate with the Word of God in his or her heart. This process helps the receiver grow in the ability to discern God's presence in his or her life in order to follow God in a more authentic way.

Another proverbial expression from Ignatius is "The devil never has greater success with us than when he works secretly and in the dark." Nothing is more liberating than when someone is given the opportunity, without being judged, to actually put into words and address those realities that have been unmentionable or taboo. Otherwise, those hidden thoughts and difficult experiences threaten to go on a rampage and wreak havoc on that person's soul.

All this presumes that someone seeking spiritual counsel can count on the trustworthiness of the spiritual director, so that whatever is confided will, without any doubt, be kept confidential, in the same manner as the secrecy of the confessional.

11

A Spirituality of the Present Moment

An Augustinian, a Franciscan, and a Jesuit all die and go to heaven. Jesus asks each one: "If you could go back, what would you change about your life?"

The Augustinian pondered and then said, "There's so much sin in the world. If I went back, I'd try and stop people from committing so much sin."

The Franciscan thought a bit before saying, "There's so much poverty in the world. If I went back, I'd try and get people to share more of their wealth with the poor."

The Jesuit looked at Jesus and said, "If I went back, I'd change my doctor."

In his autobiography, Ignatius explains how, toward the end of his life, the thought of his own death filled him with intense joy. The prospect of soon being reunited with his Creator and Lord made him "melt into tears."

At the same time, Ignatius was in love with life. He could find God in all things and serve him in every activity and event, just as his spirituality teaches us. There was no need to wait until after death to taste the joy of God's presence. In practice, finding God in all things gives us the opportunity to consider our lives here and now as the precise place where we can already experience the fullness of God's love.

Ignatius, with his genuine insight into human nature, warned against two possible pitfalls in the spiritual life: nostalgia for the past and needless dreaming about the future. It makes sense to look back on past experiences, for in doing so we can trace specific moments of God's presence. We recognize his presence in experiences of peace and joy, vitality and trust. Our past can provide a rich source of learning, especially since we can use times of reflection to inspire our choices. Such ongoing reflection gives us the opportunity to adapt our lives now so that they're more closely linked to the ways God is drawing us. But we can also get stuck in our own past and end up watching the same film over and over. Whether that is a consequence of regret or anger, the result is the same: we allow ourselves to withdraw from the only time that really exists—the present.

Ignatius did not want his novices (candidates for the Society of Jesus) to be told today what they would have to do tomorrow. That would only distract them from the great challenge that every person faces of living fully in the present moment, in the now. We can look at it this way: a good parent has to make plans for the future and do so in good time. But even in this situation, parents can be tempted to spend needless time day-dreaming about a not-yet-existing future at the expense of real life.

St. John Berchmans (1599–1621), a Flemish Jesuit who died young, understood this concept of living in the present very well. While playing billiards one day, he was asked what he would do if he were told that he only had a few more minutes to live. He answered: "I would go on playing billiards."

Trusting God and His Creatures

A Franciscan, a Dominican, and a Jesuit were playing golf one day. They were moving along the course quite well, until they got stuck behind a group of golfers who were taking a long time and weren't letting anyone else play through. Feeling frustrated, the three went up to the leader of the group and asked what was going on. He told the three priests that they were part of a special program that allowed the blind to play golf. Each blind person was paired off with a sighted player who would help him line up the shot and give him advice on what else to do.

The Franciscan was deeply edified by this display of generosity. He apologized for being so pushy, and announced that he was so impressed by this example of service that he would incorporate it into his own prayer and service to the poor.

The Dominican, too, was touched by their example, and declared that he would use this display of service in his preaching, and help others to work with those in need around them.

The Jesuit was deeply moved by their ministry. He took the fellow aside and encouraged him to continue with his work. However, he had to add one qualification: "Don't you think it would be a lot easier for everyone if they played at night?"

When Ignatius of Loyola founded the Society of Jesus in 1539, he already had a long quest of twenty years behind him. He had grown from being a conceited, vain young soldier to a humble man seeking God. After much trial and error, Ignatius had discovered the true purpose of his life: to seek and find God in all things so as to serve him more authentically with words, but more importantly, in deeds.

Most striking about Ignatius was his trust in God: "Trust in God as if success depended entirely on yourself and not on him: but use all your efforts as if God alone did everything, and yourself nothing," he wrote. Ignatius's faith in God was absolute, as was his awareness that human beings have a responsibility to participate in building the kingdom of God. Everything legitimate must be used for that purpose. "Nothing that is not in itself evil is to be put away because abuse of it is possible: to do so would shut the way to a great increase of God's glory," Ignatius wrote.

Ignatius recognized that unknown and sometimes surprising ways could help others find their purpose. Jesuits in the seventeenth century made the decision to introduce dramatic performance into their schools and colleges. They did this at a time when the Church and many others considered the theater to be a decadent, immoral activity. Nonetheless, Jesuit teachers at colleges became convinced that the pedagogical possibilities of the theater were sufficiently strong to overcome that taboo. Thus they did not hesitate to use this new means for the *humaniora* (the process of becoming more and more a human person) of the young people entrusted to them. It is important to note, however, that the Jesuits were very discerning both in their choices of plays performed and in the plays they wrote themselves.

For Jesuits, clarity of purpose enables individuals to become freer and more creative when working toward their goal. Arguments such as "we've never done this before" or "we've always done it this way" are of very little use for people hoping to become innovative.

Toward the end of his life, Ignatius was asked by a fellow Jesuit what he would do if the Pope decided to abolish his life's work, the Society of Jesus. Ignatius immediately answered that he would go to the chapel to pray to God for a new grace, and then begin working on something different. "A quarter of an hour of prayer and I should think no more about it," he said. His was the extent of his faith in God, his inner freedom, his continued willingness to pursue new paths. For Ignatius, a "means" remained just a means. When outdated and no longer relevant, he'd simply look for a different, better means to promote the gospel.

The Heart as Compass

A Franciscan, a Dominican, and a Jesuit all die at the same time and go to heaven.

The Franciscan is welcomed by St. Peter and invited to sit for a meal made especially for him by the best cook in heaven. The Franciscan thought it was wonderful.

St. Peter also welcomed the Dominican, and a whole team of heavenly cooks prepared an excellent dinner for him. The Dominican was delighted.

Finally it's the Jesuit's turn to be welcomed by St. Peter. But this time, it's Jesus himself who is standing at the stove and preparing the meal. The other two are flabbergasted and protest against the Jesuit's preferential treatment.

St. Peter explained the situation: "We are full of Franciscans and Dominicans here. But he is the very first Jesuit to arrive in heaven."

St. Ignatius of Loyola had some strong qualities, and these can often be seen in his followers. Jesuits sometimes have a reputation of being overly rational and cold, more strong-willed than holy, as St. Ignatius was often thought to be.

Nonetheless, if you read Ignatius's spiritual diary, you will notice that he was often quite literally overwhelmed with tears of joy during his morning meditation and the Mass that followed. And to add another note, Jesuits must complete their years of training with a third year of probation—a unique period of intense prayer, study, and various work experiences—and within the Society of Jesus, this final year is usually referred to as the "school of the heart."

Are we dealing with a contradiction here?

Ignatian spirituality and its view of humanity have always rested on several tensions. One of these involves the interrelationship between three human capacities: heart, intelligence, and will. Ignatius was above all a person with feelings. He led an exuberant love life before his conversion. To love and be loved occupied a central place in his life as a knight. After his conversion, that desire for love did not diminish, it just had one important difference: Ignatius had discovered that a life devoted to God made it possible for him to be more loved and to give more love in return. Therefore, by becoming more sensitive to the movements of his heart during prayer, Ignatius learned to live and act more in accord with God's love.

During his own years of growth, Ignatius also discovered that the intellect and the heart are not mutually exclusive. On the contrary, a well-formed intellect makes it possible to refine our capacity to listen to God's voice in our hearts, and thereby better able to interpret that voice. In the sixteenth century, Ignatius was forced to realize that study and knowledge provided access to networks and domains that, without qualifications and certificates, threatened to remain closed and inaccessible. And he knew that it was important for the gospel to be proclaimed in these networks and domains as well.

Understanding, knowledge, and reason are all objective. They are similar for everyone, even though one person may have a bit more of one than another. Yet God chooses to speak within the subjectivity of each person's heart. This is the most important and essential place where God's special desire for each person can be found.

So what about the will? Ignatius indeed had exceptional willpower. However, that did not make him rigid or aggressive. Until his death, Ignatius continued to listen to God's voice in the depths of his own heart and in the hearts of his fellow Jesuits. He would use his intelligence to interpret the movements of the Spirit he had discovered within his heart. He would use his willpower to take what he had learned through his intelligence and heart to make specific life choices, and then to be faithful to these choices. In this process, Ignatius understood just how our will helps us live ever more in accordance with the movements of our hearts.

Ignatius's experiences teach us that the heart, intelligence, and will complement each other—although it's always the heart that forms the compass.

THE WAY TO ST. PETER'S BASILICA? YOU WON'T FIND THAT...
IT'S JUST STRAIGHT AHEAD!

The Challenge of Enculturation

A Jesuit arrived in Rome and wanted to go to St. Peter's Basilica. He asked a Dominican to show him the way.

"Father," said the Dominican, "I'm afraid you'll never find it. It's right in front of you."

Most people have a tendency to assume that the shortest way is the most efficient. Why take a detour? Just head straight to your destination without making the journey too complicated.

The haphazard reality of human experience, however, shows us that life doesn't usually work out quite so simply. Responding too quickly is often considered imprudent or even threatening. Communicating too directly can produce the opposite effect than the one intended. After all, humans are not machines who can be preprogrammed. We must first win people's confidence and get to know them over a period of time, and doing this requires both space and time and lots of patience. Even the most exquisite main course is usually preceded by drinks and hors d'oeuvres.

In regard to the proclamation of the gospel, Ignatius was fond of saying that you should always enter through the other person's door in order to exit through your own door. We can only hope to gain true contact with someone if we are prepared to step into their "world," which may have its own language and culture. It's important to meet people, young and old, where they are and respond to them accordingly. You run the risk of being disappointed if you try to force a situation. If you don't prepare ahead of time and adapt to the life situation of the person or group, you may as well return home from a fruitless journey.

It is no coincidence that Jesuits to this day have produced many dictionaries. Studying the language and culture of a people most often becomes the first requirement for making effective contact with a new group or culture. Thus, as Ignatius teaches, you may consciously choose to take a circuitous route with the hope of finally reaching your goal.

Francis Xavier, one of the founders of the Society of Jesus, wrote about meeting people where they are in a 1549 letter to a fellow Jesuit, who had stayed behind in India while Xavier continued his travels to China:

> The truth is, that men listen attentively to those things above all which reach their inmost conscience. . . . You must show men clearly to themselves, if you wish to have them hanging upon the words of your mouth. But to set

forth what their own interior feelings are, you must first know them; and the only way to know them is to be much in their company, to study them, observe them, pray with them. So turn over and over again these living books.

15

Friends in the Lord

A Franciscan gets a haircut and asks the barber how much he owes him. The barber says he never charges the clergy. The Franciscan thanks the barber and goes home. The next morning, the barber finds a big basket of fresh bread from the Franciscans' kitchens.

An Augustinian gets his hair cut by the same barber. The barber also tells him that he never charges the clergy. The next day, the barber receives a nice bottle of wine from the Augustinians' wine cellar.

A Jesuit gets his hair cut and the barber again explains that he never charges the clergy. The next day, when the barber gets to work there are twelve Jesuits waiting for him.

It is often said that Jesuits are lone wolves, and this reputation is not wholly undeserved. It may seem that each Jesuit goes his own way instead of participating in community life. The broad diversity of activities and commitments in which Jesuits are involved only reinforces this idea of individualism.

But is it really the case that Jesuits are gentlemen living apart, yet somehow together? Or that a Jesuit house is more of a hotel, the center of their absence?

A look into the actual experiences of Ignatius of Loyola offers a much subtler view. The image Ignatius had of himself was that of a pilgrim traveling around in search of what God desired of him. Serving God and his people was the number one priority in his life; yet, however strongly he was focused on an apostolic life, he was also very much a man who treasured friendships.

In his autobiography *A Pilgrim's Journey*, Ignatius describes how he began looking for companions right after his conversion. From that moment on he tried, together with these new friends, to discover what God desired of them as a group. The decision to found the Society of Jesus was the result of communal discernment and decision-making by the first ten companions.

These ten men called themselves "friends in the Lord." The bond between them was from their friendship with Jesus, a friendship that was, in essence, apostolic. Ignatius and Francis Xavier were close friends, but that did not deter Ignatius from sending his best friend on a mission to India in 1540, even before the Pope had given his approval for their new order. Ignatius and Francis Xavier were never to see each other again. The fact that they were members of a *communitas ad dispersionem*, a community of men to be dispersed all over the world, was beyond question for both of them.

When Francis Xavier died in 1552 off the coast of China, he was carrying a small linen bag against his chest. In it were the signatures of the other nine original companions, carefully cut out from their handwritten letters. Although he had often been alone, Xavier felt himself closely connected to these Jesuit companions. From the very beginning, a wide variety of methods of communication existed among Jesuits throughout the world: through letters, from the verbal reports given by Jesuit visitors traveling around the world, from intimate spiritual conversations with a spiritual director, a superior, and close Jesuit friends.

To this day Jesuits remain a worldwide brotherhood as companions of Jesus. However great their diversity, their shared spirituality and common formation, along with their personal bond with Jesus, are what strengthen this sense of solidarity and mutual connectedness.

Their shared desire to remain "friends in the Lord" has taken on a new form among current-day Jesuits. Many of them now cross province boundaries for studies and ministry, and Jesuits who are in the same age group but from different communities meet regularly to share whatever is closest to their hearts. In addition, given the present situation within both Church and society, their experience of living together in community is very much part of each Jesuit's apostolic mission.

However, that doesn't mean that community life is always a bed of roses. The young St. John Berchmans, SJ, who was known for being cheerful and outgoing, once confided in a fellow Jesuit that his greatest penance was daily life within the community, or as he said it in the original Latin, "*Vita communis est mea maxima penitentia.*" Jesuits don't get to choose their fellow brothers. And thank God! The reality is that living together with other men, day in and day out, is a valuable lesson in brotherly love, especially in the small, everyday details of common life.

Committed to Faith and Justice

Two Jesuits were standing beside the ox and the donkey, looking down at the crib holding the baby Jesus.

One of them suggested: "This child seems to be full of potential. Let's encourage the parents to sign him up for one of our colleges."

"I was thinking the same thing," replied the other. "But between the two of us, the child is of very humble birth."

In 1773, Pope Clement XIV abolished the Society of Jesus. Jesuits were expelled all over the world. The superior general at the time would spend his last days in prison, and the Society of Jesus would not be restored until 1814. The reasons for the Suppression were complicated and ambiguous, though we now know that envy had a lot to do with it. Jesuits worked as confessors and preachers in royal courts, and not all Jesuits were equally free when it came to power and glamour.

Ignatius himself took on the role of spiritual director and advisor to a great many prominent men and women. He encouraged his fellow Jesuits to devote attention in their apostolic work to anyone holding a position of responsibility within society. Such people, after all, are "multipliers"; they make it possible for any good initiative to bring forth abundant fruit.

But the range of activities Ignatius engaged in was much broader than only working with the rich and powerful. Three years before the founding of the Society of Jesus, he returned to his birthplace in the Spanish Basque Country and spent several months there. Instead of going back to the old family castle, he stayed at a local inn, much to his family's consternation. Ignatius gave catechism lessons to street children and succeeded in convincing the local authorities to organize food distribution to the poor. Later on in Rome, he set up the St. Martha House, where former prostitutes could take refuge as they began new lives.

When the Jesuits expanded their network of schools and colleges, they inaugurated an unheard-of innovation: their education would be free. At a time when only the wealthy could afford to pay tuition, education was a privilege enjoyed by a very small elite. But the Jesuits' commitment to free education was strong. It explains why, for example, in pre-revolutionary France, about 60 percent of the students in Jesuit schools came from the working classes.

Although this social awareness has continued over the centuries, it hasn't always been followed equally across the globe.

Pedro Arrupe, the Jesuit superior general from 1965–1983, played a decisive role in reinvigorating the Society of Jesus' commitment to social justice. Under his charismatic leadership, the thirty-second General Congregation (the highest Jesuit governing body) declared in 1974: "The mission of the Society of Jesus today is the service of faith, of which the promotion of justice is an absolute requirement." A few years later, Father Arrupe launched the Jesuit Refugee Service, a nongovernmental organization in which numerous Jesuits and their lay coworkers devote their best efforts to educate and assist refugees.

The same commitment to social justice pervades most Jesuit works today. Nearly all of the 461 traditional high schools and 189 institutions for higher education across the world include social justice education and outreach as part of their regular student curricula. In the last fifty years, Jesuits set up 3,000 schools in Africa and Latin America to provide quality education for those who couldn't afford tuition.

Jesuits are required to find and serve God in all things. They also ensure that the richness of the gospel can be experienced at all levels of society. Only when Jesuits follow paths of both faith and justice do they remain true to the inspiration of their founder.

17

Learning from Our Desires

A Jesuit and a Franciscan sat down to a dinner where pie was served for dessert. There were two pieces of pie, one much smaller than the other. The Jesuit reached over and took the larger piece for himself.
The Franciscan remonstrated, "St. Francis always taught us to take the lesser piece."
So the Jesuit replied, "And that's exactly what you've got!"

Ignatius systematically invites us to begin prayer this way: Ask for what you desire. Express what you desire, what is going on in your heart, what you are in need of at that particular moment. This has nothing to do with what you *think* you should desire or feel, nor with what others think you should desire, however edifying and valuable such thoughts may be. It is all about what you really experience and desire, even if it seems to be strange, politically incorrect, or something you're not proud of.

Though asking for what you desire may sound simple, it is anything but. Most often you are barely aware of what you desire. Or perhaps you don't even want to admit to yourself what is going on deep down in your heart.

God's love can only fully reach and transform you if you are both able and prepared to open your heart up to him just as you are. If, for whatever reason, you pretend to be something you're not, you'll present a distorted image. Personal growth thus becomes an invitation to greater self-knowledge, honesty, and humility.

Another reason why asking for what you desire is difficult is the reality that you can't ask the question *and* give the answer. In other words, asking for something means you have to let go of part of your autonomy. You adopt a more dependent position and entrust yourself to the unpredictable divine providence of God. This asking presupposes your acceptance that the answer will come from someone else. Such letting go can cost a great deal, even if the someone else happens to be God. We always prefer to control things ourselves.

Ignatius invites us instead to inner freedom, to trust that the inclinations received in prayer might be very different from what you expected and may lead you toward a much richer life. Asking for what you really desire in prayer is not reserved for children or the particularly pious.

Sometimes you feel nothing in prayer. Sometimes you find no desire in your heart at all, only apathy and emptiness. Does this mean that you can't pray? Quite the opposite. It is in these times that you doubly need God's closeness and support. Here Ignatius introduces a subtle nuance. He reminds us that though you may have no specific desire at times, it is possible to "have the desire to desire." In this way, Ignatius claims that a desire to desire is itself a desire. That initial "desire to desire," however modest and fragile it may be, can become the starting point from which you can rediscover a whole new connection with the flow of life and grace.

Here's a quote from Ignatius, by way of illustration. He encourages us, despite everything, to entrust ourselves to God's grace:

> There are very few people who realize what God would make of them if they abandoned themselves entirely to His hands, and let themselves be formed by His grace. A thick and shapeless tree trunk would never believe that it could become a statue, admired as a miracle of sculpture . . . and would never consent to submit itself to the chisel of the sculptor who, as St. Augustine says, sees by his genius what he can make of it. Many people, who, we see, now scarcely live as Christians, do not understand that they could become saints, if they would let themselves be formed by the grace of God, and if they did not ruin His plans by resisting the work which He wants to do.
>
> —To Asconius Colonna, Rome, April 25, 1543

The Street Is Their Monastery

A Benedictine monk, a Trappist monk, and a Jesuit enjoyed a delicious meal together accompanied by drinks. During dessert, they reflected on one aspect of their order for which they were truly grateful.
"We have Benedictine liqueur," said the Benedictine monk.
"We have Trappist beer," said the Trappist monk.
"We don't allow ourselves to be bottled up," observed the Jesuit.[1]

In the Roman Catholic Church, there is a great diversity of religious orders, each one with its own charisma. The Benedictines are renowned for their centuries-old liturgical traditions. They are contemplative religious, affiliated with one particular abbey, carrying forward the *ora et labora*—prayer and humble work—as St. Benedict prescribed. Trappist monks are also contemplatives living in community. They emphasize the experience of living in poverty and silence. While the Benedictines have a strong intellectual tradition, the Trappists focus more on asceticism and manual work.

---

1. Based on a Flemish saying where "not allowing yourself to be drawn (tapped) into bottles" (referring to beer or wine being drawn from the vat) means "not allowing yourself to be made a fool of" and "not allowing yourself to be deceived."

Jesuits are active apostolic religious. Their monastery is the street. They regularly move from house to house, even from country to country. They don't enter as Flemish Jesuits or Chilean Jesuits, but as members of a worldwide family, a brotherhood of nearly 17,000 men who live in communities in more than 127 countries. Jesuits are often associated with education, but only one in five works in education. Even though Jesuits are considered highly intellectual, the Dominicans far outstrip them in this regard. And if a candidate longs for a rich liturgical life, he better not become a Jesuit, since Jesuit liturgical culture is, to put it gently, understated.

In his *Constitutions* (the fundamental rules of the Jesuit order), Ignatius forbids anyone to make changes to the rules concerning poverty, except to make them stricter. This primarily refers to the personal lives of Jesuits who, as is normally the case in religious life, submit all their earnings to the community and do not own personal possessions.

Throughout their history, Jesuits have boldly served the kingdom of God by employing contemporary technologies in their ministries. Today's use of twenty-first century media has had the same impact as the printing industry did for Jesuits in the sixteenth century.

You could say that the Jesuits don't have any real apostolic speciality. In the *Constitutions,* Ignatius wrote that the Society of Jesus was founded to "help souls." In practice this means that Jesuits are available to travel wherever the needs of the Church and society are greatest. Depending on the situation, Jesuits may become involved in social work, ecumenical dialogue, education, parish ministry, scientific research, spiritual direction, health care, or communications. This explains why you can find Jesuits engaged in so many diverse fields and in so many unexpected places and situations—living out their vocation on the streets.

Companions of Jesus

A Greek Orthodox Christian, a Protestant, and a Jesuit were doing archaeological work together in Jerusalem. While digging, they uncovered a gravestone chiseled with the words: *Here lies Jesus of Nazareth, who claimed to be the King of the Jews and was put to death by Pontius Pilate on the feast of Passover.*
Excited by this discovery, they quickly opened up the tomb, only to be dumbstruck when they discovered a crucified body inside.
"Oh, no," said the Orthodox scholar, "The Church and all the good things she has done have been based on a fundamental error."
"Oh, dear," said the Protestant, "The Bible, which has guided me throughout my whole life, is nothing but a pack of lies . . ."
"Wow," said the Jesuit, "Jesus actually existed?"

Most people will agree that Jesuits have critical minds. Yet they also have a strong spirit of obedience, which has the paradoxical effect of creating considerable room for trust, creativity, and personal freedom. Many Jesuits are not afraid to go against the grain and stand up for what they feel strongly about, even when their viewpoint doesn't coincide with what others might expect.

The experience of completing St. Ignatius's Spiritual Exercises has something to do with this. At two points in their formation, Jesuits set aside thirty days to experience the Spiritual Exercises in its entirety. These thirty days of quiet, private prayer are spent in seclusion, under the guidance of a spiritual director. Jesuits also devote an eight-day retreat each year to the Spiritual Exercises. This time of prayer often involves meditations written by Ignatius, and these meditations usually begin with a passage from Scripture and then a particular prayer method that Ignatius first experienced himself and later developed into a series of adaptable exercises.

The particular method of prayer in the Spiritual Exercises offers a constant source of spiritual growth that invites participants to take their personal experience with God seriously. Because of the emphasis on personal reflection during these prayer experiences—and the discernment that goes with it—the Exercises can lead participants to greater creativity and apostolic courage. This is true for Jesuits as well as for the thousands of men and women across the world who make the Spiritual Exercises in its different forms each year.

Though they're a creative and free order, the Society of Jesus is also a priestly order anchored in the Church. Many Jesuits take a special vow of obedience to the pope in regard to their apostolic mission. It is, ultimately, the pope who directly or indirectly provides the basic direction for Jesuit apostolic ministries in the service of the Church. The more you love something or someone, the more you see things as they really are. Jesuits, with their great love for the Church, are able to see both its lights and its shadows.

Within the Society there is one constant communal reality that draws Jesuits together, whatever their individual differences. When the first ten companions searched for a name for their new group, it seemed obvious to them that they would settle on the name *Jesus*. Thus the Society of Jesus was born. The experience of the Spiritual Exercises is strongly directed toward the person of Jesus. His life is comprehensively prayed over—from the Annunciation and birth, through his hidden and public life, and through his passion and resurrection. Ignatius always invites the individual to place himself or herself before the living Lord, and then discern how best he or she is being touched and uniquely called over the course of a lifetime.

The name of Jesus is to be found in the name "Jesuit." A Jesuit writes the letters "SJ" after his name. SJ stands for *Societatis Jesu*—of the Society of Jesus. Each Jesuit is a *socius Jesu*, a companion, a friend of Jesus. And it is precisely by becoming friends of Jesus that Jesuits become friends with and for one another. It is the friendship with and in the living Jesus that forms the foundation and irreplaceable cement of the Society of Jesus.

20

For Rather Than Against

What is similar about the Jesuit and Dominican orders?
Well, they were both founded by Spaniards, St. Dominic for the
Dominicans, and St. Ignatius of Loyola for the Jesuits.
They were also both founded to combat heresy: the Dominicans to fight the
Cathars, and the Jesuits to fight the Protestants.
What is the difference then between the Jesuits and the Dominicans?
Have you met any Cathars lately?

Ignatius of Loyola makes a spirited assertion about the Spiritual Exercises. He says that the Exercises make it possible for the Creator and Lord to communicate to the faithful soul, inflaming that soul with his love and praise, and guiding the person to figure out how best to serve him in the future: "The Creator and Lord Himself should communicate Himself to His devout soul, inflaming it with His love and praise, and disposing it for the way in which it will be better able to serve Him in the future." (*SE* 15, Fleming)

In other words, Ignatius asserts that his method of prayer can lead a retreatant to a direct experience of God. Anyone who has completed the Exercises understands precisely what this means.

In sixteenth-century Spain and France, such a statement would easily arouse suspicion. The rapid spread of Protestantism brought the role of the Church as mediator between God and people into question. And someone who contended that you could experience God directly yourself was considered an undercover Protestant, perhaps even a figure of the Enlightenment.

In fact, Ignatius sometimes presented himself—even voluntarily—before the Inquisition, since it was his desire to live and work within the tradition of the Catholic Church. The Church repeatedly and unequivocally cleared Ignatius and his *Spiritual Exercises* of heresy. Because the Dominicans played an important role in the proceedings of the Inquisition at that time, people have naturally suspected that there would be major issues between the two. But the relationship between the two orders is very positive, to the extent that when the superior general of the Jesuits dies, the master general of the Dominicans is the one who celebrates his funeral Mass, and vice versa.

Another misconception from this period concerns Protestantism. At its outset, the Protestant revolt was primarily a movement for reform within the Roman Catholic Church itself. Thus, the Jesuits were never founded as an organization to combat Protestantism. In truth, the Society of Jesus was not founded to be against something, but rather *for* something—for God and his people. This fits perfectly with the trust and optimism of Ignatius. It is much more meaningful to devote your best efforts to fight for something than to fight against something. It is far more fruitful that your best efforts be inspired by what gives you energy and joy than by what makes you fearful, angry, or sad.

What applies to the relationship with the Dominicans applies today to the relationship with Protestants. Jesuits work in many institutions and situations with their Protestant brothers and sisters in faith. Moreover, many Protestants now make the Spiritual Exercises.

About the Author

Nikolaas Sintobin, SJ, was born in 1962. After a short career as a researcher at the Catholic University of Louvain and as a lawyer in Brussels, Nikolaas joined the Society of Jesus in 1989. He was trained as a Jesuit in Brussels, Paris, and Santiago de Chile, where he specialized in Jesuit spirituality and pedagogy. Nikolaas has served as a school chaplain, teacher, and spiritual guide. He is now based in Amsterdam, where his main assignment is in online media. As an "Internet chaplain," Nikolaas is eager to find new ways to make the Ignatian experience more present in the digital world. In collaboration with the faculty of theology of the Catholic University of Louvain, he has recently developed a series of videos and the website www.seeingmore.org.

Also Available

 **An Ignatian Book of Days**
$12.95 | 4145-1 | PB

 **A Simple, Life-Changing Prayer**
$9.95 | 3535-1 | PB

 **God Finds Us**
$9.95 | 3827-7 | PB

 **Reimagining the Ignatian Examen**
$9.95 | 4244-1 | PB